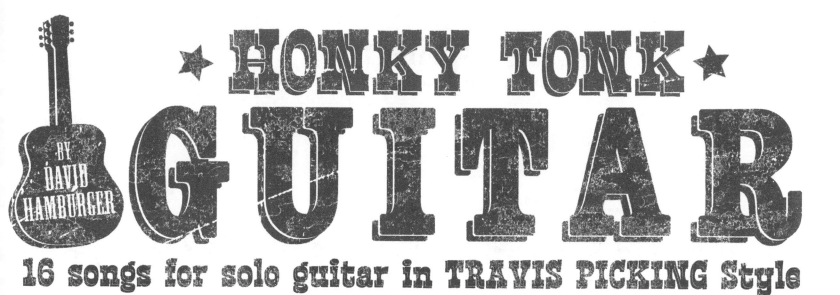

★ HONKY TONK ★ GUITAR

BY DAVID HAMBURGER

16 songs for solo guitar in TRAVIS PICKING Style

CONTENTS

ISBN-13: 978-1-4234-1147-5

HAL•LEONARD®
CORPORATION
7777 W. BLUEMOUND RD. P.O. BOX 13819 MILWAUKEE, WI 53213

Visit Hal Leonard Online at
www.halleonard.com

Abilene

Words and Music by Lester Brown, John D. Loudermilk and Bob Gibson

*T = Thumb on 6th string.

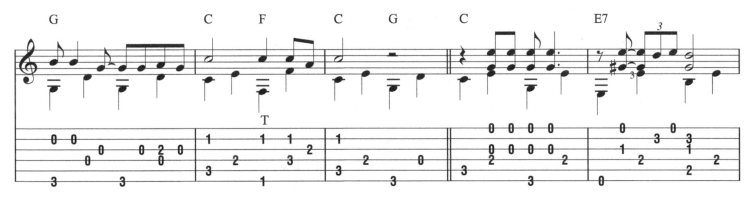

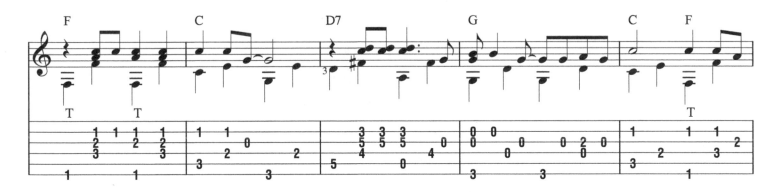

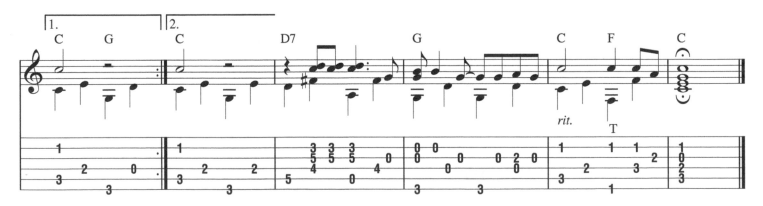

I Walk the Line

Words and Music by John R. Cash

Moderately fast

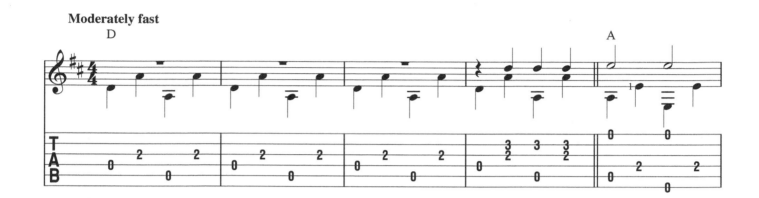

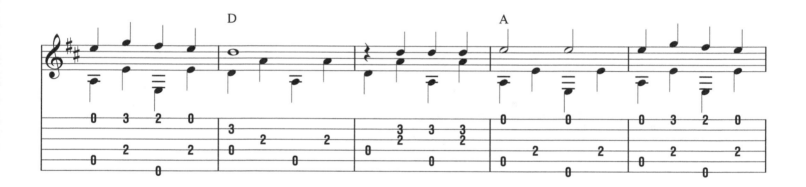

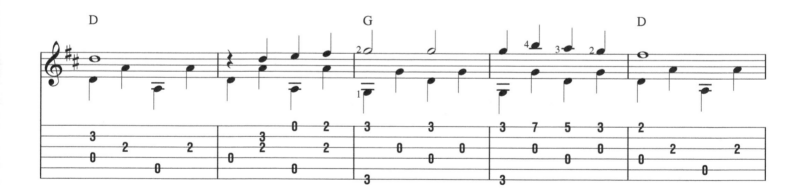

To Coda 2

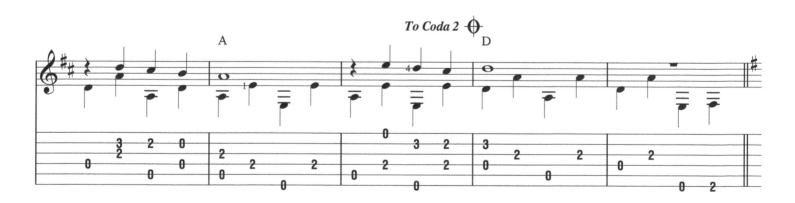

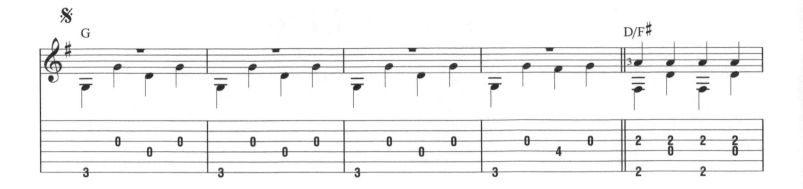

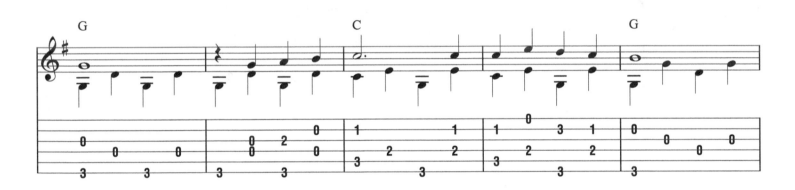

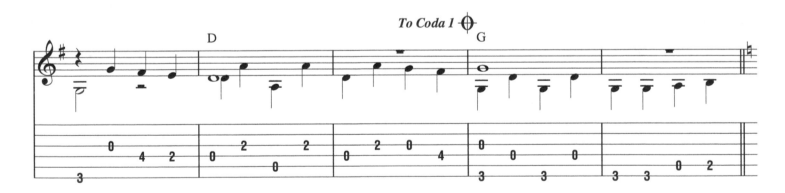

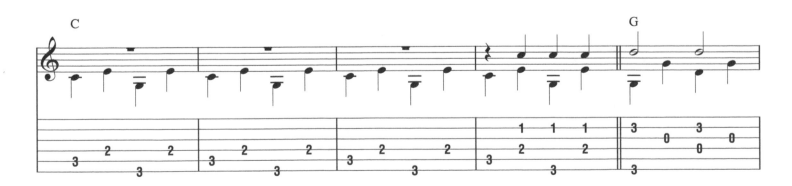

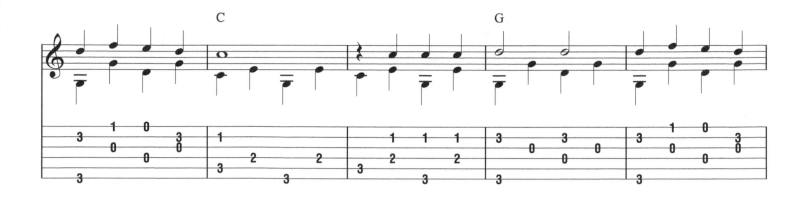

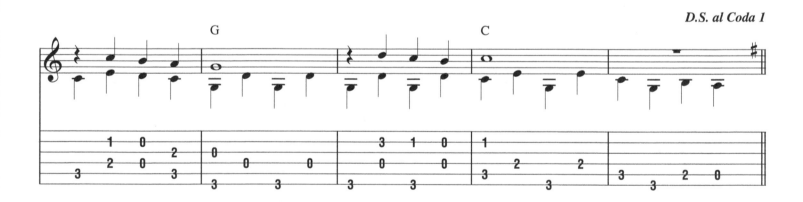

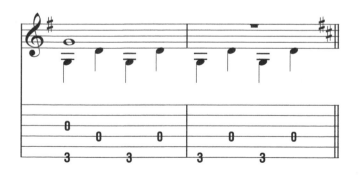

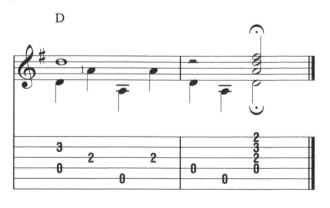

Blue Eyes Crying in the Rain

Words and Music by Fred Rose

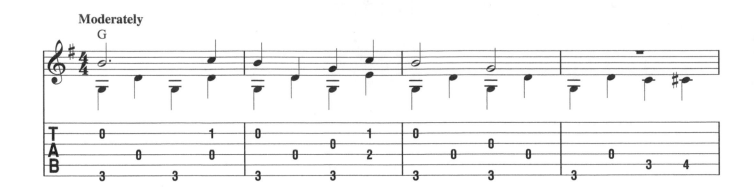

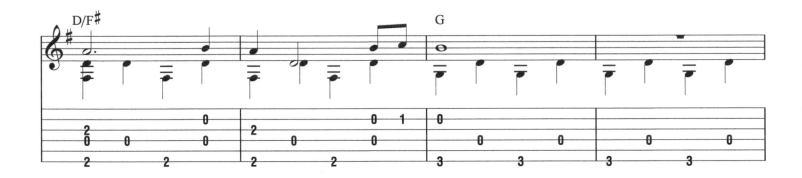

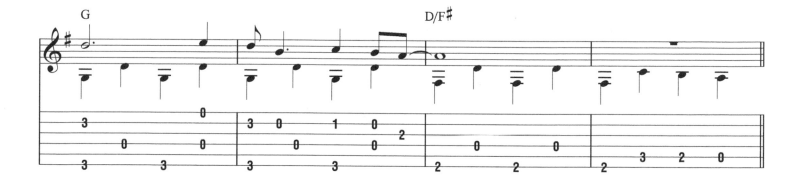

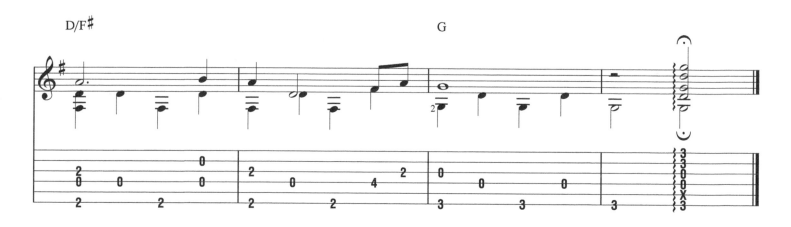

Folsom Prison Blues

Words and Music by John R. Cash

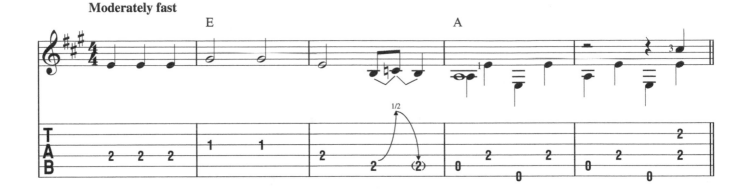

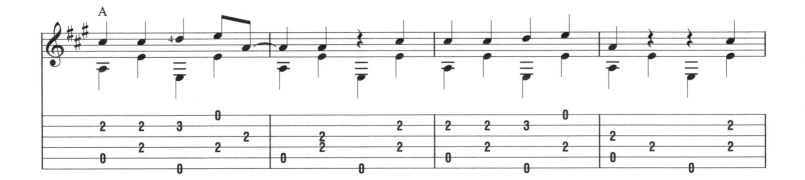

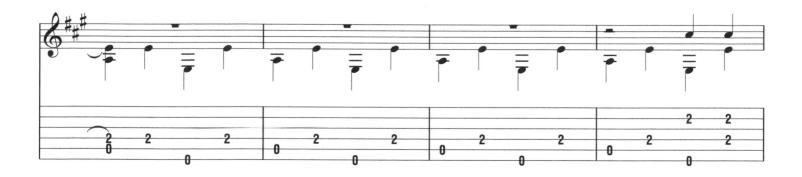

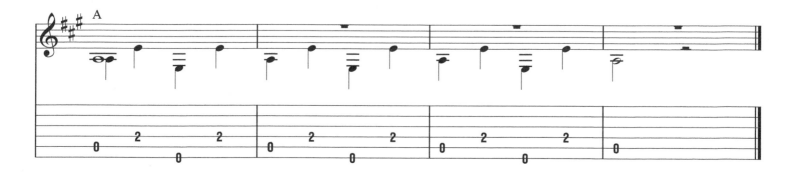

Hey, Good Lookin'

Words and Music by Hank Williams

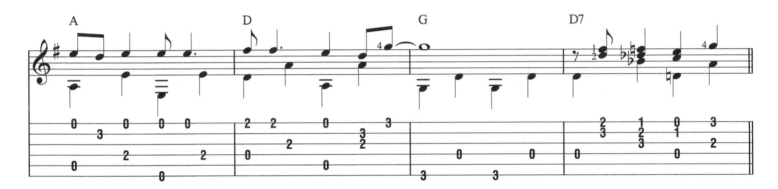

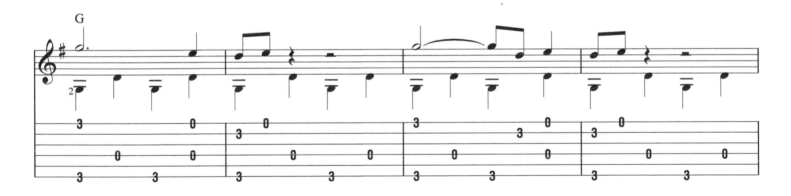

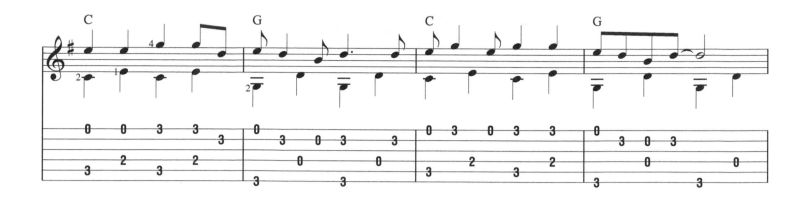

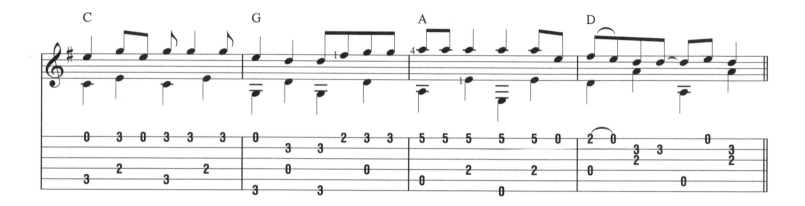

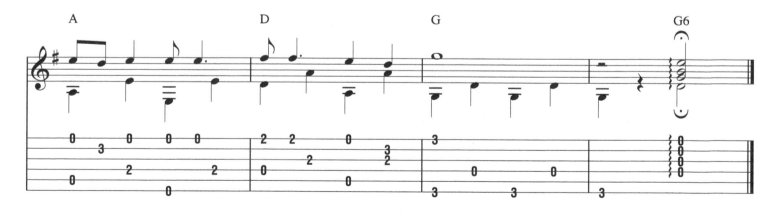

I've Got a Tiger by the Tail

Words and Music by Buck Owens and Harlan Howard

Moderately

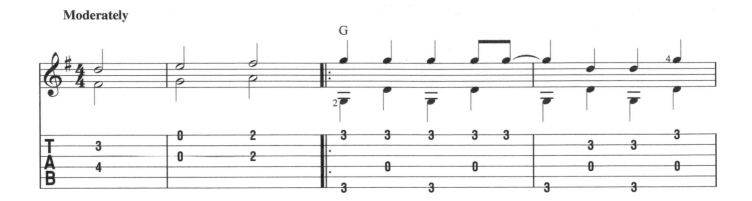

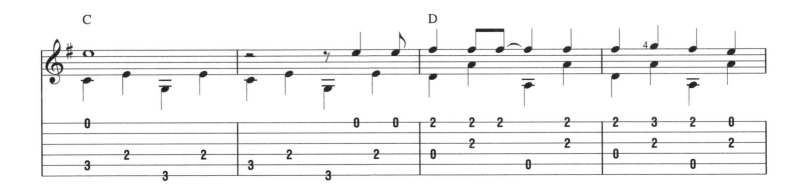

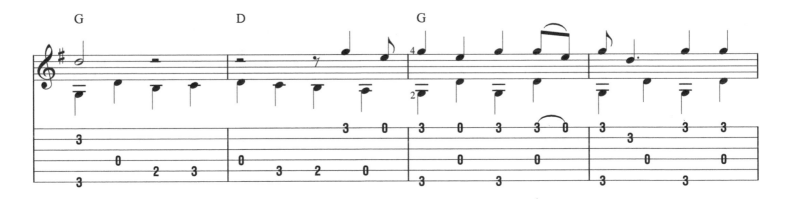

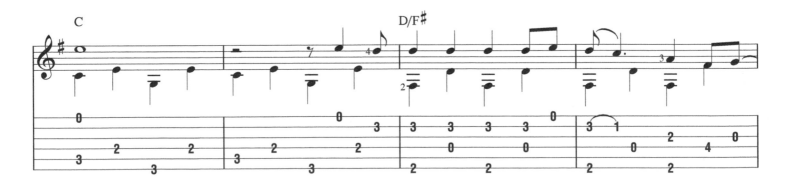

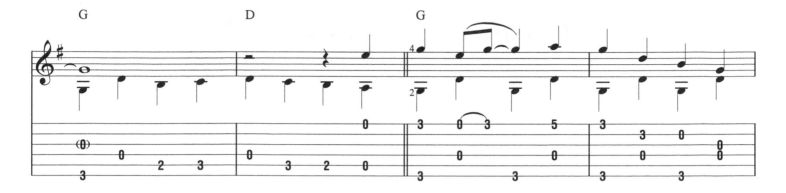

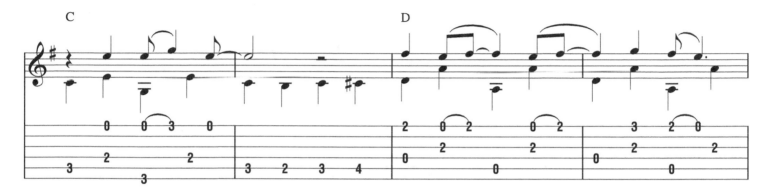

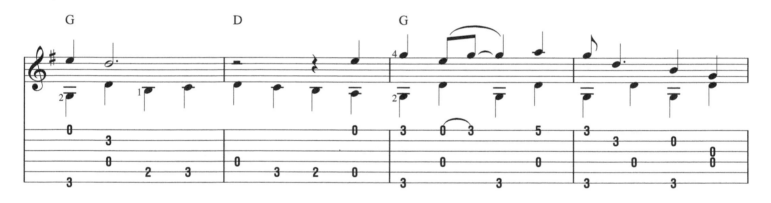

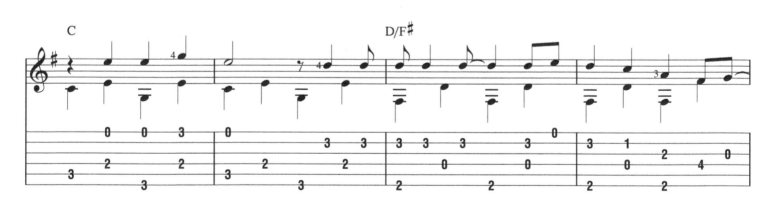

In the Jailhouse Now

Words and Music by Jimmie Rodgers

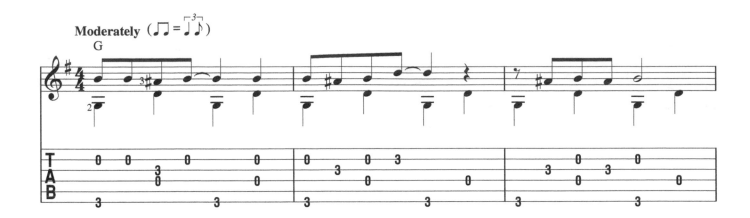

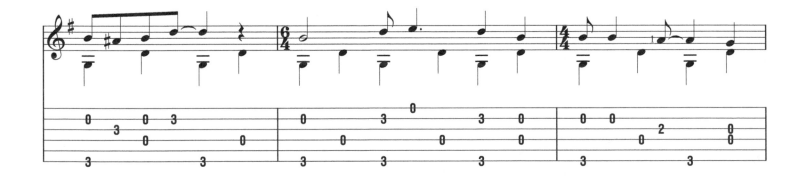

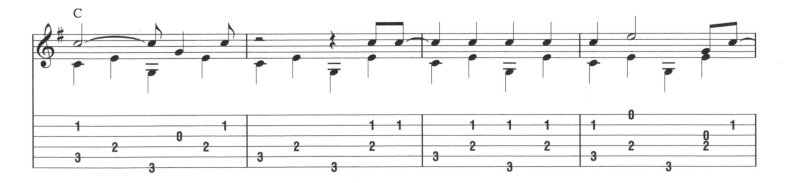

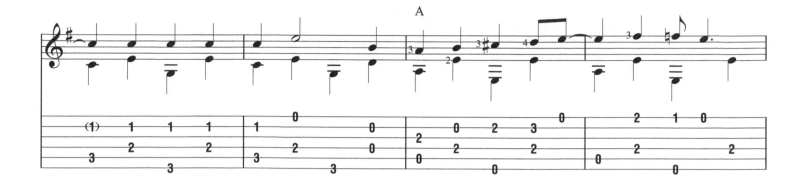

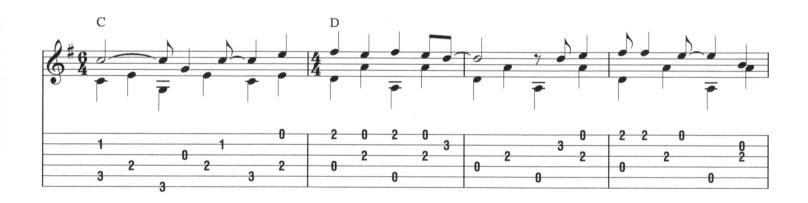

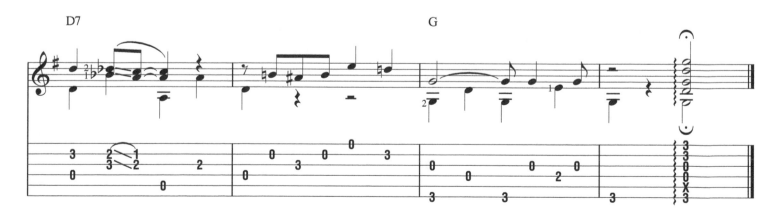

It Wasn't God Who Made Honky Tonk Angels

Words and Music by J.D. Miller

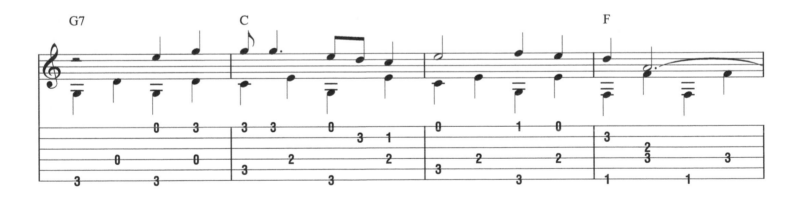

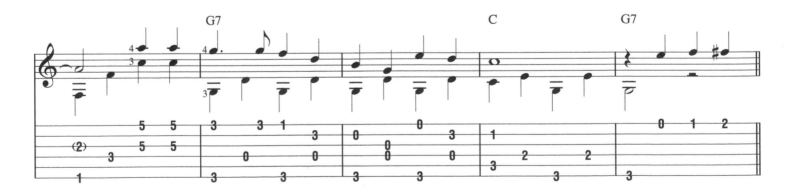

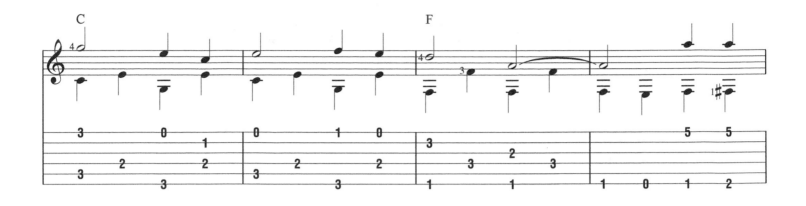

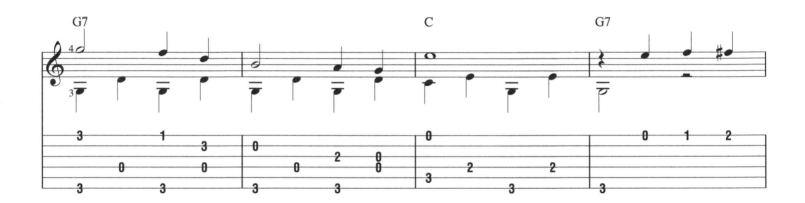

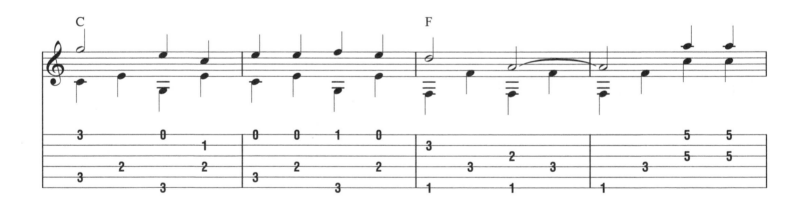

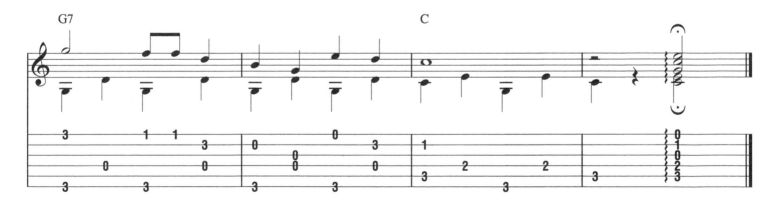

Okie from Muskogee

Words and Music by Merle Haggard and Roy Edward Burris

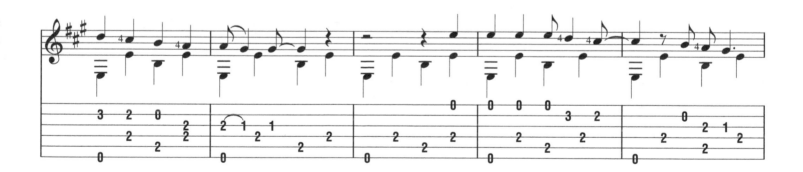

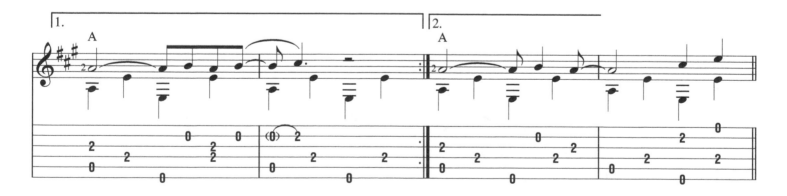

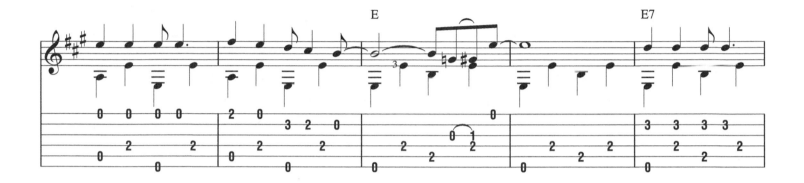

To Coda ⊕

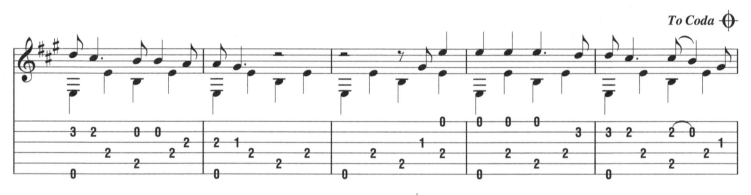

⊕ **Coda**

D.C. al Coda
(take 2nd ending)

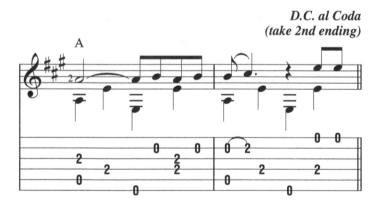

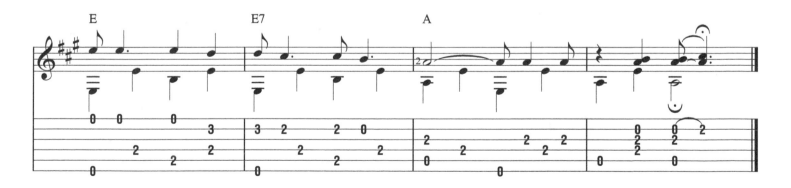

On the Road Again

Words and Music by Willie Nelson

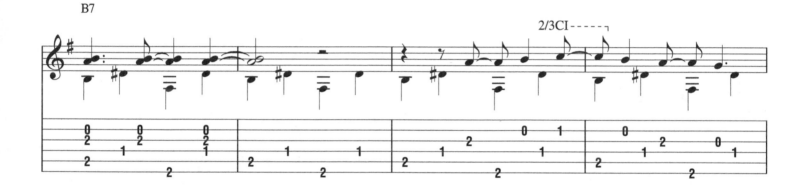

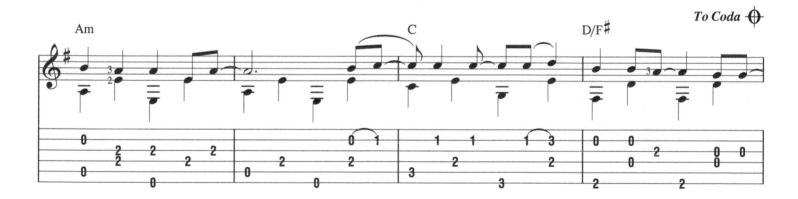

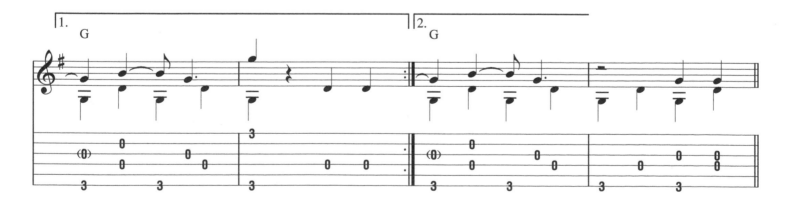

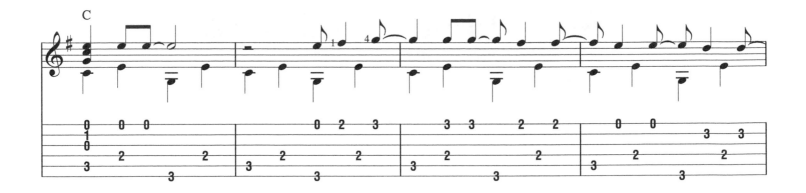

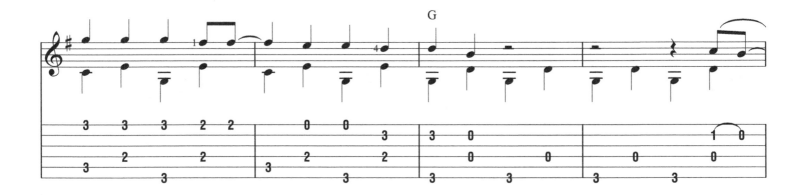

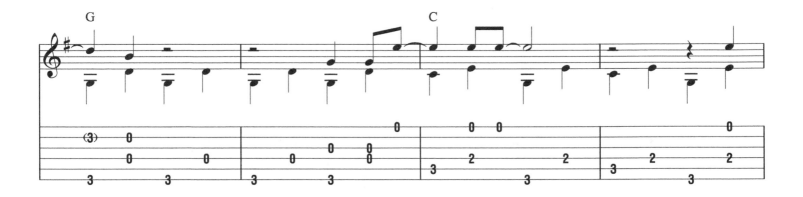

Coda

D.S. al Coda

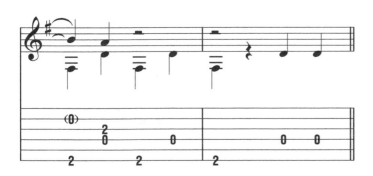

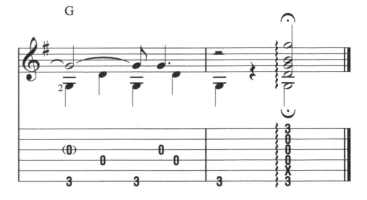

21

She Thinks I Still Care

Words and Music by Dickey Lee

Drop D tuning:
(low to high) D–A–D–G–B–E

Moderately

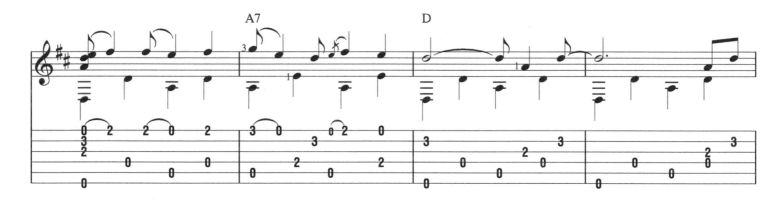

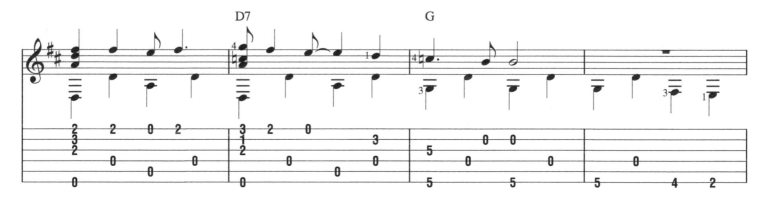

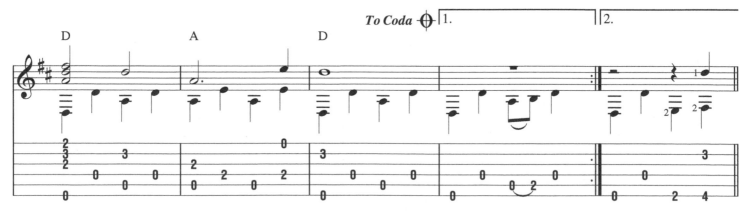

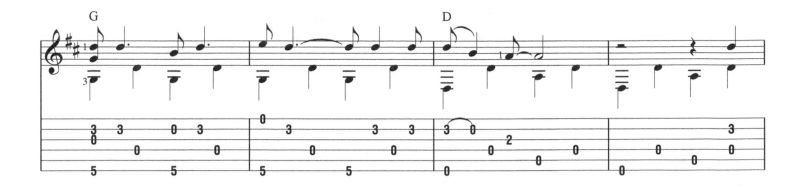

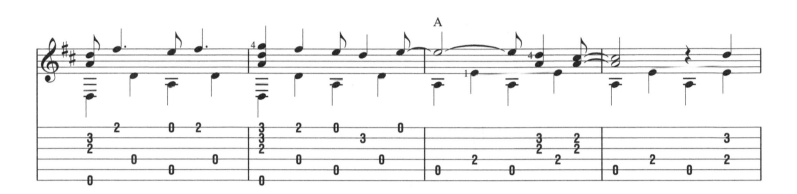

D.C. al Coda

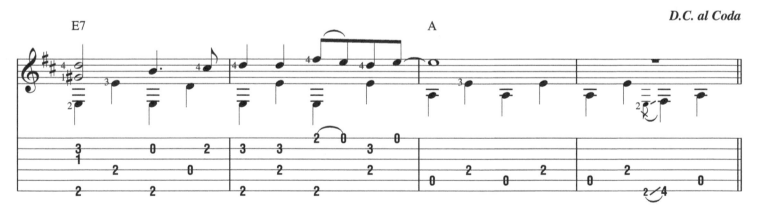

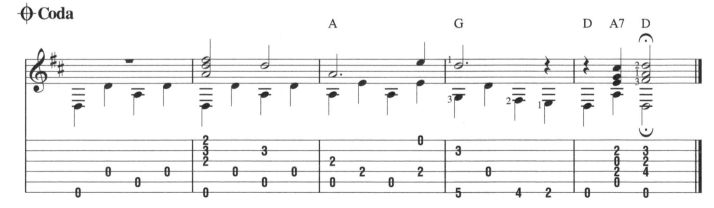

Sixteen Tons

Words and Music by Merle Travis

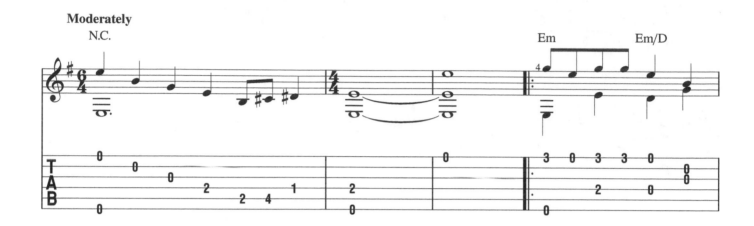

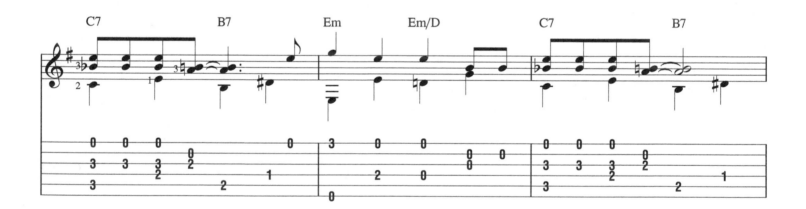

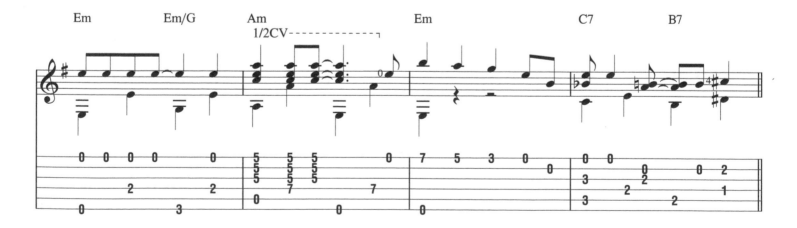

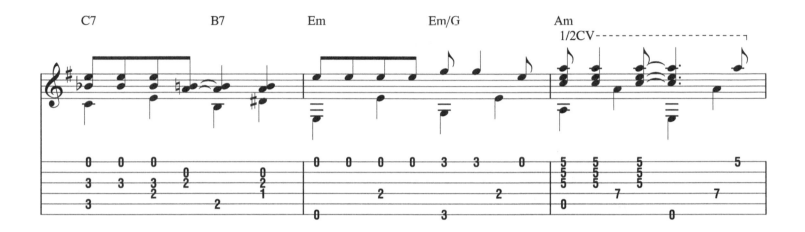

There's a Tear in My Beer

Words and Music by Hank Williams

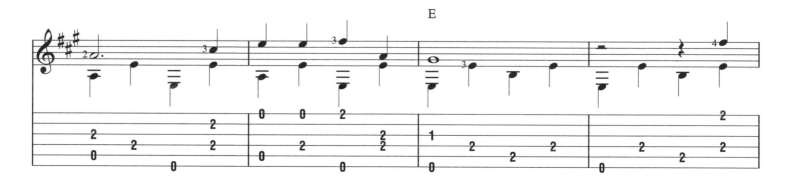

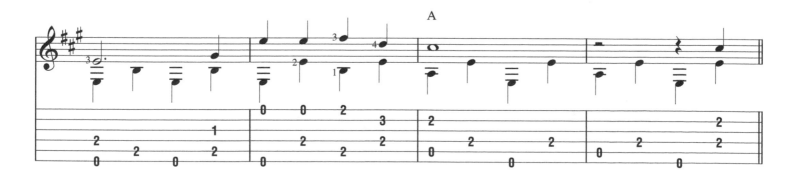

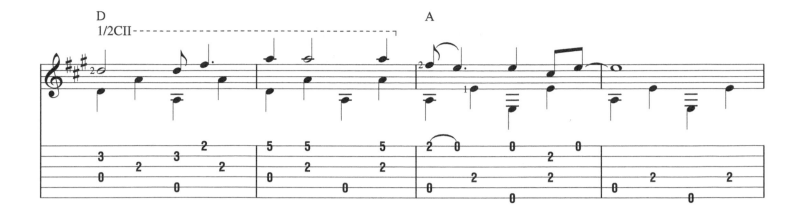

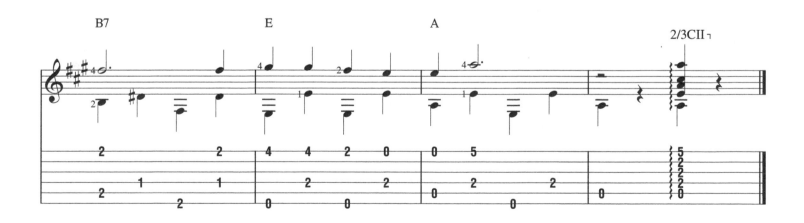

Workin' Man Blues

Words and Music by Merle Haggard

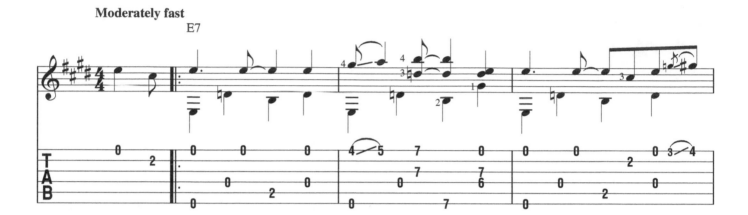

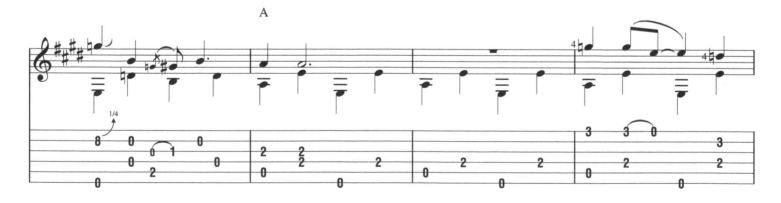

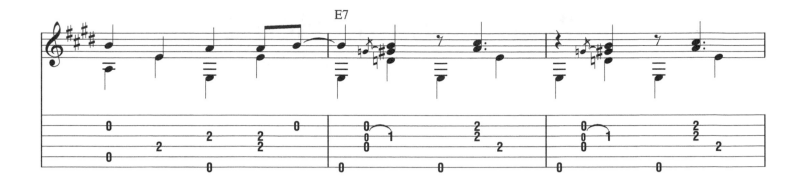

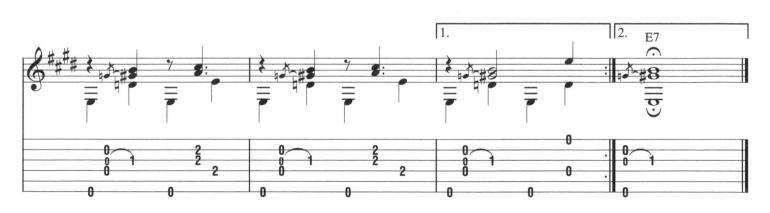

Your Cheatin' Heart

Words and Music by Hank Williams

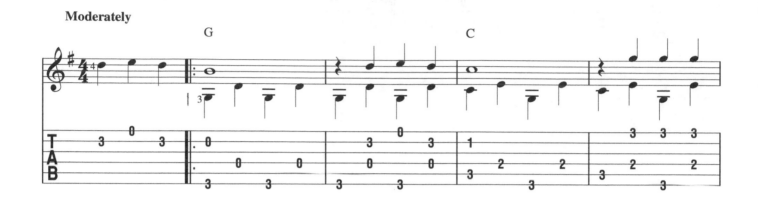

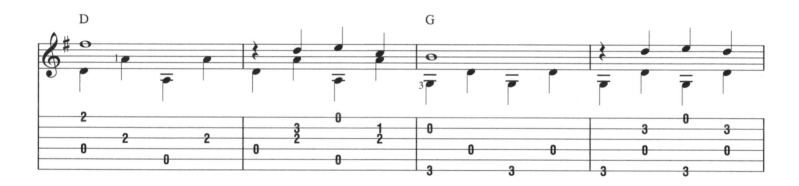

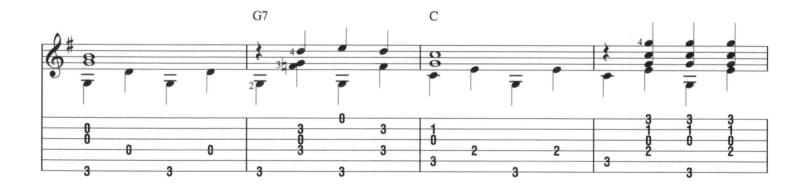

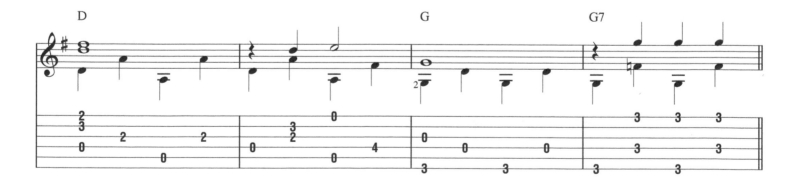

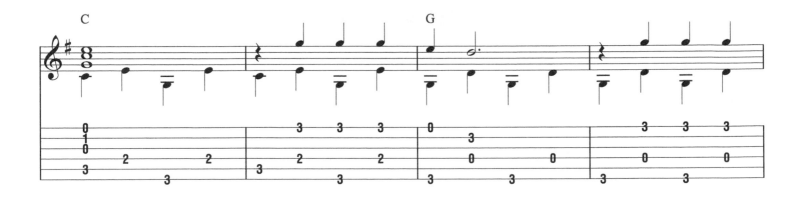

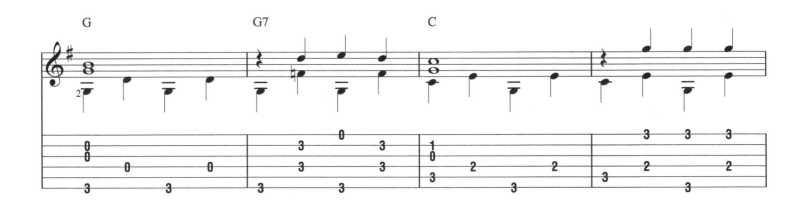

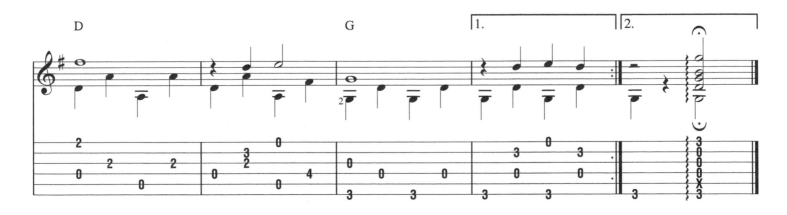

Slowly

Words and Music by Tommy Hill and Webb Pierce

Drop D tuning:
(low to high) D–A–D–G–B–E

Moderately

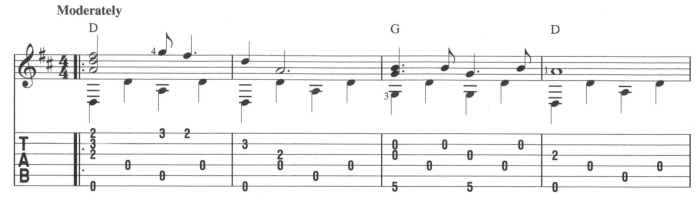

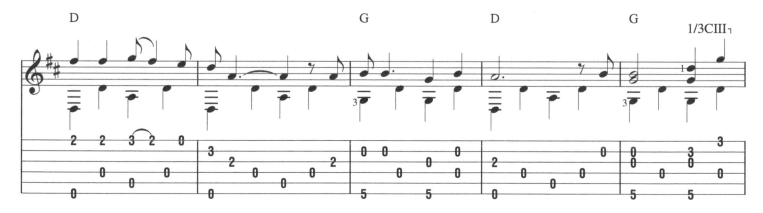

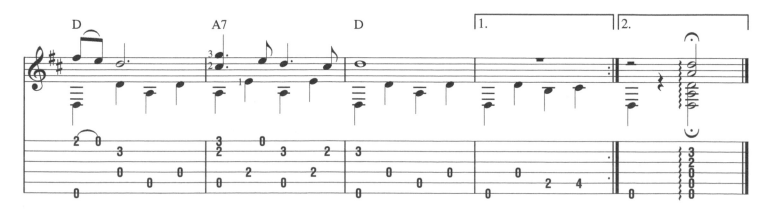